THE FALLING

PITT POETRY SERIES

Ed Ochester, Editor

THE

FALLING

HOUR

David Wojahn

For Sandra
who has the gift
of courage, and the
talent to make that
courage grow

Vermont
College 1/99

UNIVERSITY OF
PITTSBURGH PRESS

The publication of this book is supported by a grant
from the Pennsylvania Council on the Arts.

Published by the University of Pittsburgh Press, Pittsburgh, Pa. 15261
Copyright © 1997, David Wojahn
All rights reserved
Manufactured in the United States of America
Printed on acid-free paper
10 9 8 7 6 5 4 3 2 1

Library of Congress Cataloging-in-Publication Data

Wojahn, David, 1953–
    The falling hour / David Wojahn.
            p.   cm.   —   (Pitt poetry series)
    ISBN 0-8229-3995-9 (alk. paper).   —   ISBN 0-8229-5642-x (pbk: alk. paper)
    I. Title.   II. Series.
PS3573.O44F35   1997
811'.54—dc21   97-4563

A CIP catalog record for this book is available from the British Library.

To the memory of

LYNDA HULL,

1954–1994

And sang in harmony: "O founded powers
Who rule the underearth, this life of ours,
This mortal life we live in upper air
Will be returned to you. To you, therefore,
We may speak the whole truth and speak it out
as I do now, directly."

—Ovid, *Metamorphoses*, X

Contents

I

RAJAH IN BABYLON

We hanged our harps upon the willows in the midst thereof
—Psalm 137

Rajah doesn't like Nirvana but he seems
to tolerate Jimmy Cliff: "The Harder They Come"

is Rachael's little joke, and it's chuffing from her boom box
as Rajah paces, his planetary back-

and-forth, manic orbits, exactly like Rilke's
panther. The bars and his stripes run parallel

and fuse, head abob like a marionette's,
the snare drum of his paws on the cement.

He's fasted for three days, and thinks that Rachael's
brought ten pounds of horse meat in her pail,

but his flared puzzled nostrils don't smell a thing
and Noelle bends down to the tranquilizer gun

while Rachael coos endearments meant
to slow him down so Noelle will get a decent shot.

Good Rajah Pretty Rajah Big Rajah—
Eyes wide, he turns, and Noelle aims and fires

and he shrieks and circles faster and we wait
while Jimmy croons that we can get it if we really want.

"Two minutes, tops," says Rachael, and by the time
the song is over he has wobbled and gone down.

He is one four-thousandth of the world's tigers.
To save them takes some drastic measures

and so the cage door's opened and we file
in, Bob and Noelle and Rachael

and me, and the tape slurs on to "Pressure Drop"
while Bob and Noelle strain to turn him on his back,

heaving till he's sprawling belly up,
the Maytals moaning as Rachael wipes

her brow, and fumbles with the electro-jack,
a miniature land mine, a low-tech

bristle of hose and wire. The down-sheathed penis
sprouts, pink and man-sized in her rubber gloves

and now the Melodians lay down beside
the Rivers of Babylon. *Oh the wicked*

carried us away, captivity. . . . The motor's
started, the penis clamped, the tiger

bright burning, his fearful symmetry
sprawled incandescent on the scat-pocked floor. Gingerly

I touch the ribs, the whorled sleeping flank,
stutter of heartbeat, Rachael scowling as she works,

and there we wailed as we / remembered Zion.
And slowly the liquid pearls in the flask, churn

and sputter as Rachael grins. Buttermilk
gold, *and there we wailed,* it streaks

the beaker's glassy walls, brimming and bound
for dry-ice burial, for resurrection in the wild,

Sumatra and some sleeping tigress. *By Babylon
we wailed.* Applause and the Melodians

fade. The bright liquid flares. *Oh Jerusalem,
in this strange land we sing our song.*

EXCAVATION PHOTO

After making love she'd found it, asking me to touch the place
    as well:
her left breast, I remember that precisely, & just below the nipple
    I can also still recall,

half-dollar sized, a dusky pink that grew erect so often in
    my mouth and hands.
But the year, the details of the room, all blown apart in memory,
    broken vessels, potshards

gleaming in the excavation photo's sepia, sunlight & long shadows;
    & if only my hand remains,
circling, pushing, probing, *it's a lump I'm sure of it* & if
    I could tell you what would happen

next, which sound from her throat, which sound from mine, the days
    & weeks to follow
& the bitter eschatologies of touch, what profit would
    such knowledge give you?

Would you hear our bedside clock? Cars outside in the rain?—
    & where is she now? Could you tell me
that much? Sand & gravel sifted & the sought thing rises,
    stroked & circled with a tiny

horsehair brush. Bead, shard, incised bone, it does not flare
    in the toothless worker's
whorled palm; & my hand keeps moving even now, the fine
    transparent hairs

erect as they waken from gooseflesh-speckled aureole, my circles
    tight, concentric. *Do you*
feel it now? The push & probe & spiral & the sudden
    yes I can feel it too.

HEY, JOE

For Hendrix it's a sweet slow blues, Stratocaster
    pummeling leisurely the opening bars,
        a gracile firestorm that Mitchell's drums

and Redding's bass must fan and chisel, 4/4 stabs,
    the conflagration firewalling, as Jimi
        asks him where he's *going with that money*

in his hand, that *cold blue steel .44,*
    the questions almost querulous. The Leaves
        and the Byrds do it faster, lyrics slurred with shock,

and Willy de Ville implores it to strings,
    a Mariachi band, accordion-slathered to his
        lounge-lizard croon. But Hendrix knows

the song is gallows tree and killing floor,
    that death angels turn his wall incarnadine,
        definitive. The ceremonious blood.

He must take both parts—killer and chorus, strophe
    and antistrophe forged from feedback of an amp
        hiked up to ten. *Where you goin' with*

that blood . . . your hands. . . . I heard you shot
    your woman down. Fadeout and the jukebox lights
        have dimmed. And Bill shambles back toward

our table, balancing a foamy pitcher. The no-time
    of early afternoon, and Nick's is empty,
        the drinkers Dantescan, the barkeep channel surfing

until he crests on Court TV, pre-trial motions
		with the sound turned low, the nattering lawyers
			resplendent with their clipboards and Armanis,

the aging football star expressionless, jotting notes
		while a rumpled coroner aims a magic marker
			at a drawing of a face, of a woman's slit throat,

x's and arrows to mark trajectories.
		And even photos of the murdered woman's *dog*.
			"They're saving the hi-tech stuff for later," says Bill,

and I answer that the pot we've smoked
		sneaks up on you. What Circle can this be, the gavel
			flickering in the judge's fist, and Bill

rhapsodic over "Foxy Lady"'s chord progressions,
		then his segue to precognition, how Jung
			dreamed World War I, *a monstrous flood, uncounted*

thousands drowned, the whole sea turned to blood. . . ? What Circle
		where the football player's puffy, once-cherubic face
			gives way to med-lab footage, white coats

sloshing beakers, then the blurred-paisley twitch
		of cell division, fat DNA on all four TVs,
			metaphase and anaphase, beside a team

of bar-light Clydesdales? What Circle? *Where you*
		goin' with that gun? . . . How comes it now
			that thou art out of hell? Interphase,

prophase, and the whole sea foaming blood,
		pushing Mostar to page five, and bringing the dog
			who must bark through it all, the knife weaving in,

who circles and barks, manic panting against
the shouts. The leaps, the choke chain loose
against the reddened slick cement,

falling back each time until his flank
is lathered and drenched, circle and wail, his slippery
paw prints to be mapped and measured, circles

in circles, tightening, his howl against ensanguined cries,
until it seems he turns to us, his muzzle
pulsing huge from every screen, the click

of his nails as he paws at the nether world's gates.

AFTER WITTGENSTEIN

The girl is bleeding from the shoulders and the face

﹡

and writhing on the ER table. The sleepy intern gestures

﹡

and the world is everything that is the case,

﹡

in this case shrapnel and shards of glass

﹡

and an eye already lost. She's conscious till the ether

﹡

takes effect. A drive-by: shoulders and the face

﹡

ensanguined with star-shaped holes. Wrong time, wrong place,

﹡

just driving home from work. The intern fears

﹡

the glass more than the bullet holes, for in a case

﹡

like this the shards can migrate from the face

﹡

toward heart or brain. Now the ether's calming her

﹡

and he contemplates the ruin that was her face

﹡

while seeing something out of Gaudi in its place,

﹡

dreamscape, broken ramparts, stairs to nowhere

﹡

and the world is everything that is the case,

⁂

and the world has been on call for six days straight

⁂

and getting by on Dexedrine. He stares

⁂

into the gone eye and the disassembled face

⁂

and knows he sees the world's eye, its glaze

⁂

describing severed optic nerves. *And here's*

⁂

the Gorgon's seething head, the snarling face.

⁂

The world is everything that is the case.

Wreckage

Taken to a room, the yellow hallway night-light slicing dimly in, his
father in uniform & kneeling
by his bed. Bomber jacket, gold-leaf pins on the collar, & the aftershave
his father wore in those days, filling

his nostrils. *What year is this?* says the voice. *"'46 or 7."* Now his father
leads him to the dining room,
though it must be three A.M. His father has arranged it all on the table.
Some of the pieces gleam

like foil, but most are a smoky gray. *Look at them closely,* says the voice.
Describe the shapes as best you can.
And yes, he seems to lift them to his hands again, the pieces light
as balsam. You can bend

them but immediately they'll quiver back—wriggle like fish
to their earlier
shape. *Go on. You're doing fine.* Maybe fifty pieces on the table & his
father tells him how the pasture

was silvered with the wreckage for miles. He'll lead a detail from the base
tomorrow to haul back the rest.
*Pick up the largest piece. Tell me what it feels like. Run your fingers
across the surface.*

Smooth but oddly dry, a lizard's skin. His father's trembling hand. Then
he spies the lettering, the bright
symbols friezing the metal, & almost aglow. *Copy them down on this pad.
Make them exact.*

 . . . . & now again he's weeping, though he doesn't
know why. *Enough
for today,* says the voice. *I'm going to snap my fingers three times.
And then you'll be awake.*

ODE TO 196—

after Vallejo

A girl runs toward us her napalmed back in flame.
After that we practice cursive?

A girl at her desk picks the scab, her school TB test.
And now let's babble Reichian Freudian my mother naps beside me?

Involuntary memory tonsils pruned and swimming in a jar.
Do I talk now Yogi Berra with the surgeon?

And coldest winter: Plath with her ear to the oven door.
Did I switch the channel then to more cartoons?

Footage Tet and Congo Bay of Pigs. Gunshot of course to temple.
Do I meditate on gin glass, raised nine times to my father's lips?

A garbage dump in Río and a woman digging soup bones rinds.
How in the vestry do I pin my altar boy robes?

Hendrix Mekong Khe Sanh gasolined to fire.
Do I write now on a greeting card my first bad poem?

The candidate cradled, Sirhan Sirhan beamed by Telstar.
How talk of my father's future face, O_2 tank and blotches?

Matchbook on the table at Lorraine Hotel Shoot Out the Lights.
How talk now of L at nine, thirty years exactly more to live?

L in the schoolroom picks her scab and Newark snows.
And to speak now me thirteen, my first reeling drunk?

L in the schoolroom picks her scab and Newark burns.
Do I laugh now at Manson's shaved-headed girls?

Oswald in the kitchen cleaning rifle.
Do I study now Zapruder Number Three One Three?

Someone switches the channel more cartoons.
How speak of the I and not–I without screaming?

Of the I and not–I screaming in their nullifying unison?

Among the Joshua Trees

G.P., 1947–1974

Still some twilight and the fire blooms against
the smoke trees and horizon line, visible
to campers in the desert foothills seven miles away.

They pull him from the car trunk, his shroud
a nylon pup tent. Gold tequila, draining to the worm.
And the salt grains on their wrist, also glowing,

as their hits of Windowpane reach cruising altitude.
Already the pyre stings their eyes—creosote, sage, and stalks
of ocotillo that have caused their hands to bleed.

The engine idles in the headlights' shimmer
as the tape deck plays the dead man singing "The Return
of the Grievous Angel," then the reedy heartbreak of "Wild Horses,"

his cover that shamed the Stones, and they lug
the cans of gasoline, circling the pyre twice,
talking of the president's resignation

and the spaceship that crashed in Roswell, New Mexico,
in 1946, for one of them knows
someone who knows someone who saw the aliens'

silvery corpses in a secret air force hangar.
Their eyes, he says, were huge as apples.
And now the body of Gram Parsons,

OD at twenty-seven, stolen by two friends
from the airport morgue at LAX, flares and almost trembles
as the fire scalds their faces in the plaintive wash

of "Thousand Dollar Wedding," the Grievous Angel rising
in his stoned un-Rilkean splendor, rising from
the dirges of his own angelic orders,

from cinder spray and crackle as the tape goes hissing
to its final song, and the speakers cough the radio's
dead air, and the clicks of static immense, celestial.

In Memory of Primo Levi

I. SUNGLASSES

The king now saunters through the herd of sheep,
very bloated, very dead, fuzzy through balloons

filled only with ellipses. He pokes them with his riding crop,
covering his mouth with his beret. Phosgene

gas is odorless,
                        but these ewes have been dead
three days. Something kept the king in Amman

at the palace
                    longer than he'd planned
and he missed the gas shell's demonstration.

So only minions watched them bleating and go blind,
then drown on their blistered lungs' own fluid.
                                "It's timed

to three minutes," says the salesman, a bland
Canadian in seersucker, who loosens his tie

as the king's mirrored lenses hurl his own face back
to him, squinting as His Highness writes the check.

II. EXHUMATION AT POMPEII:
A PHOTO ESSAY, 1963

Mercifully, they died before the ash
rained down, huddled in a poisoned cellar,

asphyxiated prelude to Duck and Cover,
cryogenics in reverse.
                    They asked

their household deities to spare them, and this one holds
a statue of some hearth god in her fist,

along with her child's hand.
                              In the barbershop, they stare past
the pages of *Life*, to a mirrored wall and bay rum smells,

to my father shaved and wrapped in steaming towels,
cruciform and splayed. And I watch them watch me wet my tongue

to turn the page, or rise to a floor that's strewn
with the hair of half a hundred men.
                                    A breeze swells

through the open door, the hair in eddies like ash-filled sleet.
The boxcars open. The smokestacks flare against the night.

4750 Cottage Grove

The gas was used for other things, he says, delousing,
    for example. He's reaching in his backpack for some tracts.
        Don't I want to see the other side? For months

I've known he's crazy, and when he sits down to talk
    my office door stays open. . . . *no evidence that anyone*
        was killed deliberately, and his footnotes, he says,

are in the proper form. It seems the Zionist
    conspiracy reaches everywhere, to his failing
        paper grade, to the Jews and *Af-ruc-kins*

(the words almost hissed) who sit behind him in class,
    whispering about his shaven head, the drawings and symbols
        he festoons on his notebook cover. Someone's

told him to tell me every text is equal, every
    text can be doctored, every photo and document rigged,
        every witness boughten off. Just as accidents

can happen at any time, can happen, he hints, to me. . . .
    Howlin' Wolf has asked for water, in counterpoint
        to Hubert Sumlin's stinging Stratocaster.

Ask for water and you give me gasoline. . . .
    He bristles through the tape deck from forty years past
        as Christopher and I crisscross the South Side

in search of Chess Studios—what *was* Chess Studios.
    Tuesday afternoon, the streets nearly empty,
        junked cars and the projects' boarded windows, pockets

of kids in baggy pants sipping Olde English
        or scoring crack. The Wolf is singing he will
                kick out all the windows and shake out all the doors. . . .

"Did you tell him he could fuck himself?" asks Christopher.
        And I say no, I just let him leave my office.
                Kick out all the windows. . . . And 4750 Cottage Grove

is cut in two, a blood bank and package store,
        empty lots surrounding it. . . . *And you give me gasoline,*
                he growls. Real name: Chester Burnett. No plaque,

corazones de pollo butting *Instant Cash,*
        the past mere soundtrack, tape hiss. November 9,
                the anniversary of *Kristallnacht,*

and as he snaps his pictures Christopher
        gets grins or the finger from the men and women
                veering from the blood bank's revolving door,

their paths to the package store looking practiced.
        The past mere knot and superimposition:
                a row of cots, the stainless steel hat racks

dangling plastic blood drip bags, as Muddy Waters
        shrieks his *voudon* through a squat and antique mike.
                I got a mean red spider an' she's webbin' all the time.

Then the voice of Leonard Chess croaks *cut* as Muddy
        nods to Otis Spann, and it starts again,
                under layers like Troy, starts again as white-robed

nurses swab alcohol on eighteen bleeding arms.
        Real name: McKinley Morganfield, of Clarksdale,
                Mississippi. Real name: Leonid Cszwicowich,

his father dead in a Cracow pogrom. *An' she's webbin'*
    all the time. . . . Layers like Troy. Projection room
        in a Frankfurt Yiddish movie palace, Brownshirts

with crowbars setting canisters of film on fire,
    training Lugers on the firmaments
        of three glass chandeliers, naked mannequins

lugged from the tailor shop next door and tossed
    dismembered on the pyre. Photo courtesy
        of Werner Bischoff, Magnum Photographers, Inc.

Real name: fire. Real name: ash. Real name:
    memory of ash. The *this-will-be*
        and the *this-has-been* locked within each

other's arms. And I say no, I just let him leave.
    Brick through a window and it starts again. *Asked for water and* . . .
        A bulldozer sputters in August heat. The workmen

laying phone lines down have found the field of bones.

SPEECH GRILLE

She was her mother. But now she was a bride of Christ. Holy Sisters
    -of-Something-or-Other,
garbed in white linen. For seven years her mother had been there,
    a cloistered order,

three hours north of Montreal. The drive began with snow. They took
    turns at the wheel,
her husband first, barely speaking. The marriage had come apart, that
much
    both of them understood, & to tell

her mother seemed the right thing to do, though her mother had
    never approved of them.
The snow fell in thick pasty clumps, & they dreaded the thought
    of having to spend

a night in that grim town by the cloister, its dingy hotel. They waited
    against the bars & wire mesh—
the "speech grille" it was called. To touch was not forbidden,
    but only with the fingertips

& you had to strain to inch them through the wire. Candelabrum
    on the table, guttering.
Nowhere to sit, & you were given five minutes. For years her mother
    had been suffering

from cataracts, & as she approached the thick half-circles
    of her lenses flashed
in the candlelight, clumsy halos on the swaddled, wimpled head.
    She had planned

this moment for months, but now what was there to say?
      Her mother's face,
far off & refracted as the three stood silent. Then the drill & flicker
      of the fingers through the mesh.

BORDER CROSSINGS

Bottles on the closet floor,
    bottles underneath the bed.
        Of course he thinks he's caused

it all. The hiding places
    unimaginative, the vodka's
        glass sides clear when empty,

clear when full, like the cellophane
    -transparent plastic skin
        of the model he glued together

thirty years ago, The Visible
    Man, the tiny organs in
        "authentic colors," kelly green lungs

and scarlet heart. But he's trying,
    as they say, to reside in the moment,
        stuffing the duffel bag

to bring her where she's trembling
    on the ward, where she's hating both
        herself and him, passing four

locked doors to reach her, as if each
    were some frontier checkpoint
        to a country even farther

distant than the one he's trapped
    in now. The zebra-striped gate,
        the guards who hold his documents

against the light, peering through
        the watermarks and faded passport stamps.
                And he knows his skin is glass,

his mission shame, and shame
        the lingua franca of these lands,
                the sign language of fingers

unzipping compartments
        with a nylon hiss, to probe
                her sweaters, jeans, and stockings,

(the toothpaste tube uncapped
        and sniffed) and shame the notebook
                and the novels he's brought her,

riffled and shut with a strange
        and final delicacy, and shame
                the signal that motions him on.

FIVE ESCHATOLOGIES

> *I that mighty Leveller am coming, to Levell in good earnest, to*
> *Levell with some purpose, to Levell with a witness, to Levell the*
> *Hills and the Valleyes, and to lay the Mountaines low.*
> Ranter tract, 1649

I. ENVOI: END WORDS (WACO, 1993)

The SWAT team of the ATF: seven have fallen
and of course repeatedly on film, dull
and repetitious as an undergrad's sestina. Click

click, click. Someone's pitching *hair,*
a drug to grow it, tresses so bounteous
you could fill a warehouse, but this

is not how the lab coat phrases it.
Channel 20, channel 50. Common nouns
work better than abstractions: *house*

and *grandmother, stove* and *child. Almanac*
and *tears* are riskier. Click, etc., click.
Two months later and the cult, led

by God himself, or self-proclaimed
variant thereof, performs its kerosene suttee.
The pause button freezes some soap starlet's face,

lips parted wide. (Common nouns
work better. . . . *Self-loathing,* for example:
too rigid and immutable.) A doll factory burns

in Thailand. Forty women dead and now
they're dark blue phrases on a light blue screen,
software from Japan. *Factory* and *doll.* Write

what you know, which is blue screen,
never factory or doll. Now the envoi of
obligatory memory, screen inside a screen,

which is not experience, merely *screen*
though this one also is burning,
as the moneyed and unmoneyed meet

in East L.A. in 1974, where the Symbionese
Liberation Army is a shotgun house
consigned to twenty thousand rounds

of semiautomatic fire, is a shotgun house
going up in flames. The federal agents
pause to reload. (Field Marshal Cinque—

what was his given name?) And the kidnapped
heiress, rechristened *Tania*,
sits tied to a chair in a Motel 6,

seeing herself a warehouse of hair
put screaming to the torch on all three networks.
Blue screen (click). *Stove* and *child* (click).

Aerial shot of pillaring smoke.
The ABC reporter from a helicopter (click)
intoning "We can only speculate . . ."

before the chopper blades drown out her voice.

II. TILL WE HAVE BUILT JERUSALEM
(GUYANA, 1976)

The Temple colonists have slashed a road
from the landing strip to the settlement. And from
the window of the plane he watches boats

lap the docks of the Kaituna. Reddish-
yellow soil and the first crude barracks, the grids
of streets constructivist, and the pilot angles

down to land, tunneling a single tipsy cloud,
scrolling out against Diebenkorn blue.
And did those feet in ancient times . . . The plane

bumps down the gravely runway, gasoline smell as the props
die to the pilot's radio, crooning Marvin Gaye.
Humid Tomis, Jungle St. Helena, Settlement

of Pale: and thus the exiled Prince Stephen Jones
arrives, his mission to prepare his Father's way,
his legion mostly boys and bail jumpers,

who with him will clear four thousand acres,
dawn to midnight every day, felling brush and hardwoods
dense enough to deflect an iron axhead.

Bring me my bowl of burning gold . . . The method
is to leave the fallen trees to dry for months,
then streak through them in teams of two, one boy

with a can of kerosene, the other with a torch,
the fires' sputtering constellations building
to sudden white hot walls. And before them

the whir of wildlife—monkeys, iguanas, a parrot
with its wings aflame. *And we shall build
Jerusalem* . . . Tent city to beget

the barracks, the school, the hospital, gravel runways
smoothed to tarmac, shiny as new LPs.
The Tabernacle and its golden pulpit,

the altar and its dais, the PA that will boom
his Father's voice halfway to Georgetown. *And did
the Countenance Divine shine forth upon*

our clouded hills. . . . The ruined forest burns
for days. *And was Jerusalem builded here* . . .
And was Jerusalem . . . How many years ago? A vision

to smolder down decades for him. *O Clouds unfold* . . .
So that his face for the first time brightens,
the reporter nodding as he hesitates and speaks

again into her tape. *I will not cease from Mental Fight* . . .
Running hands through his hair, he stubs his cigarette.
We'd come in with bulldozers, and push the embers

*in ravines . . . and the coals would hit the soil and explode
like fireworks.* Their hair, he tells her, was always singed,
their faces black with soot. *And did you love your father?*

*Yes. . . . And was your father mad? . . . Yes. . . . And can you
forgive your father. . . ?* He turns his head from her,
hand pressed to the window and the cartwheeling

implosions of Toronto snow, the tape's soft
steady hiss, the click in the silence as it
reaches the end. *Bring me my spear. . . .*

O Clouds unfold. . . . Bring me my Chariot of Fire.

III. RESORT AT PLAYA GIRON (CUBA, 1992)

The trigger pull of flip-flops on the Bay of Pigs
Where Danes as pale as canvases by Malevich
Parade fat torsos on a white sand beach.
Someone's shortwave blares the Pogues

From Key West or Fort Lauderdale
As six Yemeni women test the waters
In the chain mail of full-length Lycra *chadors,*
The husband shadowed by a beach umbrella

Flaring in the wind with his burnoose.
A wall divides us from prying locals,
Socialismo O Muerte neatly stenciled
On stucco topped with wire and broken glass.

Daiquiris by the graves of "revolutionary martyrs,"
Machine-gun fire of ice in dueling blenders.

IV. ON THE SUPPRESSION OF RANTERS
AND THEIR LITERATURE:
THE HON. JUDGE RICHARD BAXTER, 1649

Their tracts were burned, and many killed by Publick
Hanging or the stake, by decree of His Lordship
The Protector, Oliver Cromwell, for the worke
Of Satan and His Hostes doeth never stoppe,

And Heresies and Heretickes He makes
To thronge like Locustes from the bottomless pit,
Numerous as the caterpilleres of Aegypt.
For the Ranting Power is a devouring beaste,

And in one booke it reades they claim that God
Is as much within an Ivie Leaf
As in His most Glorious Angel, that the Quick and the Dead
Shall all anon be judged. With torches the bailifs

Now make their rant part true. The pyre burns:
Thus saith the Lord, I Overturn, I Overturn.

The apocalypse is here right now, the woman says,
  though in Spanish it must sound more terse. This
   in an *autopisto* rest area, like you'd find

in Ohio, though the parking lot spills over
  with campasinos, machetes in butcher paper
   sheathes. Two hundred miles to Havana, and she's hitching

to her mother's village, while telling us
  how everyone *knows* Fidel has warheads
   and will use them on his own: *Jonestown para*

ocho milliones. Cienfuegos tonight,
  where the four-lane ends, Spanish for
   one hundred fires. And beyond the rental Nissan's

smoked gray windows, the cane fields whistle by,
  already slides, clinking against
   the fins of antique Chevies, bust of Che

scowling from salmon balconies, various
  ocean sunsets, crimson as the face of the cop
   we'd picked up fifty miles ago (for only

turistas have gas), puffing up his jowls
  with an impression of his Russian
   colonel in Angola, cheeks inflated

as a cartoon pig's. The churn of Kingston reggae
  fades to Miami stations — *the fixed stars,*
   all just alike as lack-land atoms, split

apart, and the Republic summons
    George Herbert Walker Bush to a Dallas podium,
        acceptance speech gauzed by static, against

Radio Libre's pyrrhic hiss of counteroffensive:
    sixteen Cuban Golds in Barcelona.
        Thus saith the Lord, I overturn,

I overturn: the Ranter Abiezer Coppe,
    writing from Newgate Prison. The fields shuffle by,
        and sure as posthypnotic suggestion

I'm buoyed to October 1962,
    missile trajectory charted in a drawing
        in the *St. Paul Pioneer Press,* mother pointing

to its caption—how the missiles when in place
    will target as far as Hudson Bay. Wire service
        photos: alligator-briefcased Robert McNamara,

horn-rims agleam, Fidel sandbagged in a gun emplacement.
    Tonight, the Columbus Day pageant, *four playlets*
        composed by the students of Wildwood Elementary

to commemorate the Age of Exploration.
    I still have the photo of myself as Cortez,
        tinfoil helmet and an apron for a cape,

the plastic Zorro saber with a chalk stick
    on its tip, which soon will pierce the savage
        heart of Montezuma. All day I will be Cortez,

telling her I must *stay in character,*
    a flourish of slow veronicas, capework
        at the IGA, where she's taken me to fill

the station wagon with canned goods, batteries,
water for the fallout shelter. The stock boy shades
his forehead, peering skyward as he slams the trunk.

Truth-Taking Stare

. . . in which generally the patient has the sense of having lost
contact with things, or of everything having undergone a subtle
but all-encompassing change, reality revealed as never before,
though eerie in some ineffable way.
—Louis Sass

Or gallery. Or strange askew museum. Or painting of a hotel bed
with some cheap print above the headboard. (Palm tree or a sleigh
pulling Xmas trees.) Or the day two-dimensional, subzero

as I run the beach along the frozen lake. The waves
lathed to Hokusai spirals. Cold gallery, every inch
of wall space covered, park benches derbied by snow.

House designed by Frank Lloyd Wright. House for battered women.
House of the servants of His Godhead Reverend Moon
Who plots in some Seoul penthouse His glorious

death and resurrection. Ten minutes ago I left you
to the laying on of hands. Maria talking fast in glottal
Polish, and the physical therapist, hugely blonde,

lifting your legs, white cocoons of the casts. First up,
then to the sides, the hospital bed in the living room
hulking, whirring as it moves along with you.

To talk of this and you directly, though I can't.
To heal you with my own hands though I can't.
Legs not working, hands not working, tongue encased in plaster.

The tongue going numb with the hands. Why my friend Dave
loves jazz: to hammer and obliterate the words,
nullify too the wordlessness. "Blue Train" on my Walkman

as the Moonies leave from house to van, lugging crates
of silken flowers. Blue pills that didn't work.
Then my month of yellow pills. To not metamorphose

to my father writhing as the charges surge
from temples down the spine, a dog's twitching legs
in sleep. To mollify with acronyms: ECT, Odysseuses

and Tristans of PDR, yellow Prozac, sky blue Zoloft.
To heal you with my own hands though I can't.
The day two-dimensional. (Past and present and to dwell

in neither.) Truth-taking stare. Height and width,
no depth. On a screen the paramedics ease you
from car to ambulance, having labored with a crowbar

at the door, and I push again through the crowd
on Thorndale. *This is my husband. Please
let him come with me.* The inside of the ambulance,

overlit. Not a scream, the mute button pushed.
Generally the patient has the sense . . . To watch
the memories shuffle on a screen. To Portugal ten years ago.

Our Lady of The Wordless Stare. The Bishop of Leiria
in sepia on the gallery wall, his hand that waves
a sealed envelope. Caption: "The Famous Third Secret of Fatima."

The visitor's center, thronging with white habits.
The road to the Basilica flanked by tourist booth, a wax museum.
Faces of two nuns who point to every photo, who've fled Cambodia,

one who speaks some English, and the beautiful younger one
whose tongue was "excised" by the Khymer Rouge—
on pilgrimage, thanksgiving for deliverance.

Their charter bus from Nice is parked outside,
pneumatic door and motor humming. Our Lady of the Wordless
stares at me. She stares. . . . And I'm shaken out of it

by helicopter stammer, drowning Coltrane,
all sixteenth notes as the Moonies reach the left of the frame.
Dissolve, myself, from the right of the frame. Synesthetic

whir of chopper blades, six hundred feet above the lake.
Then the picture empty. And the lake with wind anointed.
And the lake with wind. And the emptiness, anointed.

II

THE SHADES

I. PETER AT THE PSYCHOLOGICAL CLINIC, 1908

That Peter lit a cigarette was evidence
of a something-like-human intelligence.

He'd dressed himself, and laced his roller skates,
donned a child's tuxedo and
a starched cravat.

Doctor Witmer placed him at a small
three-legged stool. Told to spit, his spittle

found his shoe. Told to spit elsewhere,
he aimed at the table.
A screwdriver

was given him, and with it he opened a box.
But the writing test showed *a considerable lack*

of success,
though with some effort the missing link traced
a *W* on a slateboard, which he then erased,

hurling the board to the floor—tabula rasa—
and scowling at the chalk dust on his paw.

Kamala and Amala, raised as wolves.
The Wild Boy Victor,
    his body hieroglyphs

of scars. Wild Peter, kept as a kind of pet
by Doctor Arbuthnot, associate

of His Majesty King George, of Pope and Swift.
Imagine their guttural chorus, for none *do have the gift*

of language, which distinguish man from beast
(Arbuthnot).
    From his throat only cries do emit,

which seem to me selfsame, whether he doeth whimper
after flogging or when begging for his supper.

My wordless father in a basement, a rifle to his mouth.
Inhale, exhale, synapses drilling a forking path

to *trigger* as action, not speech. A flurry of cries.
Inhale, exhale.
    There are no words for this.

III. CHORALE 2

My wordless father in a basement a rifle in his mouth
My father wordless in a basement a rifle in his mouth

My father a rifle in his mouth
                    wordless in a basement
A rifle in his mouth my father wordless in a basement

A rifle in his mouth in a basement my father wordless
In a basement my father
                    a rifle in his mouth wordless. . . .

Inhale, exhale. The weeping that brings her down the stairs.
The weeping that asks her
                    to take the gun away, his hair

fallen down in his eyes, the salt sting synesthetic,
so he *hears* the bitter taste, is blind as much as mute

until the paramedics come to "talk him down."
Mute but weeping
                    in a backless cotton gown

on the sixth floor ward, the call button, the Thorazine,
the locks and straps to make him safe again.

Erase the hundred and forty syllables.
Erase their grids and lines. Cancel:

fadeout to pre-Guttenburgian cry,
                                          unverbal
as snow on a speechless field. Cancel:

fadeout to the cellar where Kasper Hauser huddles
in a synesthetic half-light,
                                          guttural howls,

bread heels flung through a slot in the door. Cancel.
Fadeout. My father in the locked room lying still

as a scowling nurse
                          brings his white paper cup of pills.
He's scarcely breathing, face turned toward the wall.

Not a jumpcut: the film itself unspools,
celluloid melting, or ribboning the floor, subtitles

blurred. *Describe this empty screen.*
                                          Opal? Pearl?
Cancel. Cancel, fading like a vapor trail.

At the barstool Dean gulps down his Rolling Rock
as liquid circles stamp the counter, our talk

dead fathers, veering to side effects—how Prozac
makes the mouth dry. Our talk dead fathers who never spoke

and sons who do,
                    inheritance of guilt
we can never talk to death. The dream last night—

white room and a cot, my father with a voice box
stapled where his larynx was, the choke

and wheeze of static from its speaker. His eyes
take me in, accuse. . . .
                    And now we rise

from bar light to the snow-pocked North Side streets,
the ice-slick platform of the el, the door's pneumatic snap

that opens to a nearly empty car, to the chatter
of the deaf-mute couple—
                    their gloved hands rise and flicker.

Even here in hell, the strict Virgilian grandeur,
the cellblocks of the dead in fluent hexameters,

Cocytus and Styx, Tartarus and the Vale of Tears,
and here Aeneas meets his ghostly father—

Aeneas advancing toward him on the grass,
He stretched out both his hands in eagerness

as tears wetted his cheeks. . . .
                              And now his father's tedious
prophecy, the cavalcade of heirs, of Romulus,

the double-plume of Mars fixed on his crest,
all clumsy as a wax museum tableau vivant.

But it's the smaller, unheroic stuff I underline,
fatherless and heirless both:
                              and there he tried three times

to throw his arms around his father's neck.
Three times the shade
                    untouched slipped through his hands.

VII. FORT SNELLING NATIONAL CEMETERY:
ST. PAUL, MINNESOTA

Thirty thousand dead, the markers all identical,
and with a map I find his stone,
                                    find my own name chiseled

here between the monoliths of airport runway lights
and "the world's largest shopping mall," its parking lot

nudging the cemetery fence. The spirit in its tunnel
does not soar, the spirit raised by wolves.

The parable of the cave, the spirit raised
by shades and flickering shadows.
                                    Down the grid

of colored lights a Northwest triple seven
lumbers into sleet
                    that melts against my father's name

like the striking of a tongueless bell, a code
compact and unabstract as DNA, and with my hand

I trace three times the rough, wet letters.
The jets shriek
                    and the rain-slick marble shimmers.

III

THE NIGHTINGALES

*We may listen to the music they sang, but the sound is not the
same; the Italian way with the knife is gone.*
  —A. J. Dunning

I. SOCIAL REALISM: CEAUSESCU ODE

Thy father being drunk the day he named you
Nicholae. Thy father drunk the day
he named Thy brother Nicholae, and the day

Thy sister Nicholina named. But now Thou art God.
Great Leader Great Economist Great Helmsman.
And now Thou art seven stories of bronze

which gesture in a greatcoat from a traffic island
lording central Bucharest. Domitian and Trajan
and the crapulous prestressed concrete

apartments, cloned by high-rise Soviet thousands.
The inns where you stayed turned shrines.
Thy cigarette stubs encased in glass

in the People's National Museum.
Great Hero Great Guerilla Fighter, Barehanded-
Slayer-of-the-Fascist-Horde, Wehrmacht helmets

cobbled beneath Thy feet Homeric.
Suliman Darius Cyrus Offa, the Mighty Impaler Vlad.
To sing not of the partisans, stopping to reload

Klashnikovs, having videotaped Your groveling demise.
To sing instead Thy Palace and Thy Chocolates
girdling strawberries star kiwi fruit, dulcet filling

of Cointreau. Thy dais and Thy Seraphim
Gestapo Host, who hover iconic
beneath Thy throne, their raiments golden.

Of Truncheon and The Coffin-Sized-Cell,
of Sodium Pentothal, of Electrode-on-the-Testicles.
O Ba'al O Marduk O Indra O Jealous God

Panopticonic. Huge Eye Our-Very-Eye.

The chair himself will introduce the speaker, his eyes
reptilian on the crowd.
                    The Foucault toady shuffles papers

while the chairman notes we're "undertheorized."
Our Foucault minion's flown from Yale. He chatters

about *power* awhile. Chaucer and power. Marlowe
and power. Dryden, Khomeini, and film noir

and power.
                    The wire-rims shine, the shaved head glows
like platinum. With a flourish he sips water,

necromancing as the Q and A begins.
(Bio-power. Power and Knowledge. Power and Will.)

Sixteen tweedy sleeves fly up in unison
like footage caught by Leni Reifenstahl—

to prove we are not undertheorized.
Dribbling brie, the chair unscrews the jugs of wine.

III. OF CAPONS

The laser scans the aria, his voice's luster robbed
by age, by digital transfer from another century.

The hairless capon's face, sepia toned,
looms out from the CD:
                              Alesandro Moreschi,

the end of the castrati line, the last
Tiresias, his balls an offering to the Muse.

Naples, 1842, and the boy's just passed
his seventh birthday. The "Man with the Knives"

is found and paid. The parents fidget outside
the barber's room. The boy's placed in a bath.

The barber's whetstone sings, the boy anaesthetized
with opium.
                    Easy as pulling a tooth.

He'll trill his way north, from poverty and Naples.
His showpiece:
                    The Love Cry of the Nightingales.

IV. HYGIENE, 1959

Alcohol and baby oil and cotton swabs. They peel the tiny foreskin back. I'm turning from their faces to the wall, the Davy Crockett bedspread pressed against my cheek. Every week for seven years, the only time they'd ever touch me. Mostly I recall the sting, the smegma-crusted swab in clockwise circles on the head. They never speak through this. Mostly the sting. She turns the swab and dips the clean end in the alcohol *(The ur-dichotomy—love and power, love and shame, the alpha and . . .)* He runs his fingers through my hair and on she works. Mostly the sting. Though sometimes a warmth beginning there, to radiate down the legs or up the spine. The quivering, pre-Cambrian erection—which makes them halt, let go *(Do I remember that they scowled?),* and wait for it to pass. She moistens the swab again. The sting again. The swab, the sting, the fingers through my hair.

And now he can only touch himself, awkward
as a marionette. His wooden arms flay.

The puppeteers lean forward from the dead,
spectral and paternal. And now this play

within a play. The image of a thrashing starlet
replicating moans.
                    Perfunctory foreplay,

then the image of a silent man's ejaculate
empearling slowly her breasts and face.

Slo-mo, fast forward: how it thrills the marionette,
this clumsy sleaze Perrot
                        whose heartbeats race

as fast as the clicking videotape
winding itself against itself, winding itself

to a final snap, the cough as the spooling stops
and the screen
                goes gray with static snow. *Enough.*

VI. EXPULSION OF THE DRONES

after Rilke

Lord, it is time. The huge summer gone,
You overlap the sundials with your shadows,

and you bless these deaths: two thousand drones
who have not floated skyward,

                       have not joined the elect

for their airborne copulation with the queen.
The hive shall open and you bless the deaths.

From the honey-dripping cells they're pulled and strewn
along the grass to meet their starving fates,

though some the manic workers sting
repeatedly.
               Their whirling hymn, the ground abuzz,

the apiary skyline of the hives,
my uncle's farm. I'm six: a magnifying glass

in hand, I watch the stingings' ebbs and flows.
Your offering, Lord: fifty jeweled corpses in my glove.

VII. THE SOLITARY VICE

(A HISTORY OF SEXUALITY, VOL. I)

Not the proper subject for a subject. The subject the winter of a fortieth year. *Historical singularity*, and his hands from thirty-two years past, his hands that pull my hands above the covers. *I know you were touching yourself.* ("We will not be able to free ourselves from it . . . except at considerable cost. . . . an irruption of speech . . . nothing less. . . . a transgression of laws. . . .") *You were touching yourself I know.* ("The market value of repression . . .") To chatter about power awhile. Not the proper subject for a subject. How she let me sleep with her those afternoons when he was gone. The dark patch glimpsed beneath her girdle. Something they wore, during that era. Forgotten pet names, diminuitives. The inside rush of blood. The subject the winter of a fortieth year. The subject: you can talk now, of eras. When I do it I am polyphonic but alone.

The childless only child, the end of the family line.
The fingers of the child, tracing the letters of their graves.

The wound, the source,
                     all that he blames on them.
When the child awakes, he wakes alone.

When the child writes he writes to their photos, framed
on his desk, the child who ends the family line.

The words erupt, obsessive as a nursery rhyme.
Now his *words* are touch. (They scarcely touched him then.)

The wound, the source, all that he blames on them.
Scarcely touched, touched only in shame.

He slept with her but they scarcely touched, trained
to childlessness
                 the only child, end of the family line.

Snips and stitches and the ring of foreskin's
gone, shed like a lizard's skin, and bandaged

he wakes to the spinning room: nothing to blame on them.
This vestigial umbilicus. He's seven and it's gone.

We shall not all sleep but shall all be changed. . . .
Gone the child, gone the family, set in lines

like wounds.
               Sourceless: nothing more to blame on them.

IX. THE SHAMPOO

How long it must have been, the girl's hair,
    cascading down her shoulders almost to her waist,
        light brown and heavy as brocade: the story I'm

remembering of N's, remembering as my own
    hair's washed and cut, the salt-and-pepper
        cuneiform to frill my barber's smock.

Arts and Science is expanding. The wall
    to the empty shop next door pulled down
        and a dozen workmen slink improbably

on scaffolds butting the dusty ceiling,
    cacophony and plastic tarps, the whirr
        of drills that mingles with the dryers'

jittery hums, the scissors' flash,
    veronicas of clicks, the coloring, the curling,
        the antique cash register,

melodious with its chime. And best,
    the liquid gurgle of hands massaging scalps
        the row of sinks, twelve hands and six

wet scalps in a line. I'm next, and leaning back
    (let me wash it in this big tin basin,
        battered and shiny like the moon)

to the hiss of warm water cataracts
    and Andrea's long fingers. But I'm remembering
        the girl in N's story, the girl

she was at six. This is Birmingham,
    1962, Rapunzel-tressed girl
        whose parents are more glimpsed than known,

the Family Romance, mid-century American-
    style, the child fetching ice
        for the father's drink, the far-off lovely

scent of mother's perfume. More glimpsed
    than known, separate phantom lights
        edging from beneath closed doors

those nights she couldn't sleep. Not the Birmingham
    of sit-ins, the firehoses trained on
        placard-waving crowds. But the Birmingham

of Saturdays when Anne-Marie would arrive
    as always on the city bus by six,
        before the parents' cars would pull away.

Then the cleaning until noon, the cooking smells.
    And then the big tin basin filled
        at the backyard faucet by Anne-Marie,

the long brown fingers in the child's hair,
    the water sluicing, warm from the garden hose,
        the soap suds almost flaring, the fingers

ten spokes over scalp and basin, their paths
    through the hair and down the child's back,
        the synesthetic grace notes of the hands,

the stitchery, the trill, the body electric,
    the fingertip pressure exquisite as it sings,
        the braille of *here* and *here* and *here*.

IV

ELEGY AND PERISPHERE

I. SILVER AGE

The heroes of the Silver Age stare back
from thirty years ago,
                         peering at the boy

gazing out the window to the lake
in summer, transom open, the tiger lily

patch, nodding below in the Marshes' garden
(Alsatian bride,
                  from a war called Great,

and scarcely of this century, forgotten Verdun
and Paschendale).
                  On the lake the sails flit,

moth wings. Silver Age: though the crucial metals
are higher on the periodic chart. A bite

from some plutonium-irradiated
spider,
           or gamma rays bombard the astronauts,

giving birth to the Other in the shape
of Spider Man, the Thing, the Human Torch.

II. AFTER MONTALE

"Around us, as far as the eye can see,
the inequality of objects, persisting

insensibly. . . ."
                        Spider Man versus some new enemy—
Green Goblin, Princess Python, web slinging

to triumph over Vulture, the exact
green shade of his feathers, indelible.

Sails on the lake.
                        Dog days of August
when the refugee doctor who cast my broken elbow

(hairline fracture ghostly on his fluoroscope)
dives from the inboard, having chained his hands

to a concrete block, or Private Eddie Stanhope,
the town's first Green Beret,
                        boards a transport for Khe Sanh.

Aquaman, Atom, X-Men, Thor the Mighty.
"Superman's Mission for President Kennedy."

A ramp to the golden planet of the Perisphere,
upon which several figures make their way, and one

must be my mother. The New York World's Fair,
a halcyon and edgy June of '39,

the awkward Kodak peering from its frame,
my desk:
    Nite Shot frm Italian Pavillion

with some blurred and spidery cursive on the edge. She's come
from Minnesota with her sister and three friends

to attend the future.
        Caption: "GE House of Tomorrow"
with its frozen quik-thaw dinners and an aproned

robot maid. "Good evening, ladies. Hello
Hello,"
      an amplified parrot's voice. The dishwater churns.

How radiant tomorrow was. Caption: *how beautiful.*
The summer Fermi's U235 goes critical.

IV. SUPERMAN'S MISSION FOR PRESIDENT KENNEDY

The young president sits rocking-chaired within
the Oval Office, inside a cartoon panel

with the Man of Steel, his "Physical Fitness Spokesman."
He waves a glossy of John Glenn. "No *muscle*

gap among our astronauts," the chief intones.
Panels, frames, puns, debris.
                                 Thirty-year jump cut

to Sotheby's—cosmonaut artifacts on auction
for hard Western currency. Gagarin's space suit,

a bowl once lapped by Laika, the premier dog
in space. Ivan Ivanovich, the pale

and strangely grinning mannequin who logged
a year in orbit before plunging to a Ural

valley.
        Retrieved on a sleigh by the KGB,
he's propped under kleiglights, still smiling stiffly.

Ruby fires and the assassin crumbles. Stunned
Texas rangers flicker past in black and white

before it starts again, twenty frames a second, Stetsoned
heads bobbing as the suspect writhes and shrieks,

as Cronkite for a third time points out Oswald
on the blood-slick floor,
                              beside another screen

where the curtain-swelling Minnesota sky is cold
gunmetal blue, where November sleet careens

along the panes. The Justice League of America
struggles with Lex Luthor at the center

of the earth, trapped in a valley of crimson lava.
And as my mother weeps
                              the panels blur.

Sleet falls all the way to Dallas until the center
of the earth has frozen,
                              the gunflash over and over.

VI. APPRAISAL AT MOONDOG'S

Their condition: neither Mint, Near-Mint,
nor Very Fine, merely Good to Very Good,

which cuts their value 35 percent.
The buyer makes two piles
                    and shakes his head,

a jeweler's eyepiece bobbing at his neck,
incongruous for a kid who's half my age,

a silk-screened Manson snarling from his T-shirt back,
press-on tattoos (knife-in-heart),
                        three days faded

to the same anemic red my Human Torch
and Flash are dying in, conditions flickering

from a once-Mint blaze to the cinders of Fair.
                              He searches
price guides and we go on bickering.

Then the flash of lurid green,
                    the twenties on the countertop,
each bill set down with a practiced trapdoor snap.

VII. INVOCATION: THE MUSE OF MEMORY AND THE MUSE OF HISTORY

Always fused to one another, never speaking.
By turns scratched film of a Saigon monk in flames,

or indulgent as a sick child's mother taking
soup trays from his bedside.
                                        To split like atoms,

haywire symbiotic orbits. The photo book she opens
as I shiver under poultices and quilts.

Yellowed pages even then:
                                        perispheres, pavilions
shimmering from half-life countries scraped from maps.

To split like a page bound with grids and panels: a comet
bound for earth, stylized flames on left, Green Lantern's

masked face on right. Her death beyond some vanishing point,
years to travel, subatomic.
                                        Always fused to one

another, never speaking. . . . Too late now to invoke.
Shimmering pavilions in the dusty book.

V

PRINT MADE WITH INVERTED CAMERA
IN SITU

(ca. 1893)

There was a certain pride connected to the work,
so often the police photographer survives

through a name etched on the plate,
though the victim's name and story have been lost,

the dossiers burned some fifty years ago. Neither cry
nor threnody, and in these lands there are no

spaces of exclusion—even our corpses
require surveillance, no one to evade the vast

unblinking and incriminating gaze. And here the conceit
proves perfect. Here the pyramid meets the eye,

an eye fixed to a tripod: you can even see
its wooden leg on the upper right, beside the dead woman's hat.

Almost an aerial view, a God's-eye-view
were God all and only eye, Great Lord

Panopticonic. And what, Dear Lord, does Thy image
here register? She has fallen, artless, forward,

the hallway so narrow it can scarcely contain
the black expansive foliations of her dress

splayed above linoleum, its pitted rosettes.
The right arm is beneath her and the left

flares out akimbo, the face in profile
pointing, also, left. Do You dwell then, Lord,

within these details? Within the shoulder
and its small half-moon of pooling blood, within

the stained half-opened palm? And this handkerchief,
tucked daintily inside her cuff, was it bloodied,

then, *before* her fall? By which
of Thy numberless hands did she topple, and where?

Which tenement and year, which Bayard Street
or Paradise Park, which Five Points and which

snaking warren of passageways? What stink
of smoldering creosote and garbage and what tongue —

Yiddish or Italian, Lithuanian — in her head
as her eyes glazed over? And why O Lord did Thee

place upon her head this *hat*, this cumbersome
fedoralike affair, broad-brimmed, and banded

with, no doubt, the silk of two weeks' wages?
Affixed so snugly, the fall has tipped it

barely askew. Is this then to be read
as mercy? To die, at least, in the most

exquisite Sunday hat? Could she ever speak?
Ever, in the dead-light record

of these fragments, not avert her eyes?
Why can she never return Thy stare?

Great Lord Panopticonic tell her.
She was not there when You planned this earth.

GOD OF JOURNEYS AND SECRET TIDINGS

Eurydice is better off in hell.
Isn't that what Rilke says? Hermes
guides her back, unspools black gauze
to shroud her anew, and Death again is merciful,
is grave goods, unguents, clove-scented fluids,
his lips pressed deftly on nipple and thigh,
the god's long fingers, his laving hands, their slide
as they stroke and roil and spool her shroud.

And how, indeed, could such beauty be borne,
except by the shoulders of a god? Here on the dome
of hell it rains, and you are six months' dead.
The answering machine tonight spins down—
February's messages, a half year unerased,
another mistake to tally. And on them is your voice.

FOOTAGE AND DIRGE

The rescue parties and the coroners will leave

before first snow. Return it to cornfield again,

stubble-free, some bits of metal glinting in the sun,

without the pulsing sirens, the hapless bereaved

who stagger back and forth through hail, in wind

out of Hardy poems, faces gauzed by video cams—

"they *vaporized*. . . . a thunderclap but hardly any flames."

Then the witness trails off to knee bends

in a health spa ad. How my plane bucked, touching

down at Midway—same instant the other plane fell,

but since you've died I've grown immortal.

I am the empty field. I am the field sleeping.

The workers on their knees in hazmat gear,

stabbing with trowels, combing the soil like hair.

DIRGE SUNG WITH MARIANNE FAITHFULL

The heart laid siege upon too long. The heart
imploding starlike on its violent chambers.
Dope-sick, booze-sick, heart-sick heart, cliché

and creaking ruby-colored rope. Piaf-throated heart,
its whiskey trill, noosed tonight against the notes of
"Madame George," its plundered ravishments

and ventricles. The heart most shut and always
the heart most naked, inward-traveling heart,
and always away from us. Heart in the form

of a single spot, the Bottom Line in Nineteen
Eighty-something, though her hair's still golden,
impossibly long, and the song remains

her ravaged "As Tears Go By." Her *Sing about me*
when I die and I'll come back to haunt you.
Cliché and ruby-colored rope: when I hear her I can only

feel terror; when I hear her I can only
think of you. It is the evening of the day.
It is memory and the coffin-narrow bedroom

of the rented house in London, and the figures that I can't
make out, one of them strung-out and shivering,
are you and I upon the lambent sheets. And you

still living, though the thread that bound you there
was not my arms, not my fingers that stroked
damp hair, but only "Strange Weather," then again

strange weather, bass pulse, cymbal-brush slur, her growl
and wail trembling the tiny speaker, yellow ember
of the tape deck's dial, over and over, bristling through

our dream-rinsed sleepless night. Let me leave this place,
your voices' dual necromancy, mingling of tenor,
lament and rave: fetal with the shakes,

punctum of the needle marks, blue ellipses
laddering the arms. Let me leave this place
unhaunted, love. How sad the inward-

traveling heart. How sad the heart when it has won.

Death and the Maiden

Fluoroscope: a sort of thrumming when
    the *medico* jiggles the switch. This
        I remember exactly. No lead robe, no shield.

He's settling a liver-spotted hand
    on hers to guide it to the screen
        and I can see the glossy bones of both

their wrists, fingers kinetic, fossil fish.
    Cicada-call thrum. *Move your wrist,*
        please. Upward. My eyes transfixed

on her hand, so that little of the room
    comes back, though I seem to remember
        storms that day and all that week,

tall French windows, rain-swept paseo.
    And also down? Yes. I do remember
        something of the waiting room, how she

nudged me and pointed to his magazines—
    all of them in German. Then his white smock,
        cranium shiny, hairless as Nosferatu's.

(Just the right age for a Nazi in hiding,
    she told me later in the zinc bar.
        Didn't some of them—she was

laughing now—escape to Spain?) *To the screen,*
    please. Closer. Refrigerator hum,
        initiates chanting om. *Upward, upward.*

I want to see how the arthritis . . .
      long exhalation of middle C . . .
            limits the movements of the wrist.

Don't you ever write about this,
      she said to me. (Human remains:
            I expected white sand, wispy cigarette ash,

never gravel pocked with bone.
      How quickly the lake would swallow it.)
            Then his hand on hers again,

digits impossibly long, a starfish
      wriggling a child's palm. Now the probing—
            reluctant, abstracted, everything

patinaed silver. Wristwatch, bracelet,
      wedding ring. The ghostly fingers bend, so slowly
            that her knuckles seem to creak.

ODE

Not the current century of hair; never the benighted tresses shorn by
    buyers
in the little pueblos, smuggled north; nor of course the warehouse rooms
    of it, glazed pewter

by Zyklon-B; nor my mother at St. Joseph's, & the chemo's slow
    razoring,
curls fallen, threshed; scalp left patched with a little down; & not the
    lasering

Vitalis stink on the fat mortician's hands, comb bestowing my father's
    final part,
shellacking the wave in place, freezing the breaker; nor the yellow whorls,
    entessellated cunt

still glistening in memory, our rented place in Kentish Town, street noise
    & our cries still hovering,
& both of us alive. Never this, never this, never this. Instead a room in
    Rome or Hampstead where we stared

upon the locket endlessly, enfoliated with the strands of Fanny's hair.
    Thirty-seven strands, for I
have counted them, in the glass & in the glass case for the glass. You
    were there with me.

You were there with me, gazing on the locket. Then out to the drizzling
    Heath & May the Twelfth,
1988. Whose century now is this? What home then did we make, what
    love? My face,

my tongue that parts the secret mouth & cry & roil & finger, clitoris read
    like braille,
& side by side then on our backs, swallowing the lucent thrall of air, a
    single wiry strand caught on my tongue, o glowing coal.

LULU IN XANADU

Louees you can make up some little steps here can't you?
—G. W. Pabst

That year Dirk was taking bear-gall and a powder made
 from rhino horn,
                    custom-prepared by a Chinaman herbologist.
          Through a short metal straw he'd sniff it
like cocaine. You see,
     he couldn't get it up,
            not much at least, though sometimes
I could tie him to the bedposts and
     administer a few good wacks
on his posterior and back
                    using the riding crop he'd bought me
          (all very fin de siecle) and in time
I could bring him off,
     though always with my hand or some
          pathetic little dribble down my neck. But I've gotten
ahead of myself.

          You were asking about
Mr. Hearst and Marion,
                    and the sad puny fucks with Dirk
for the most part happened at San Simeon,
     though we kept it from Mr. Hearst,
disapproving as he was
                    of sex outside of marriage.
Except of course with his Marion. The problem was
     that Marion
               got miffed at poor Dirk
who each half-hour would excuse himself
     from the banquet hall's big table
and in the john snort up his rhino horn.

84

Humphries the black servant
caught him there, told Marion of course
        and Dirk was never brought out again.
                        He never thought to explain,
mind you. Better to be thought a coke fiend
                        than an actor with his looks going
and a tool gone out on strike.

That was, I think, the beginning
        of the end for Dirk. He was up to his cravat
                in debt, and owed it to some pretty
shady characters.
                        Yet in spite of everything
you couldn't help but like him, that manic little grin,
        the way he'd hum Hot Seven songs,
                slithering in his Cord up Highway 1.
                        And to think he'd ruin his life
merely for the sake
        of a stiffer pecker, for his awkward pride.

And believe me I know what it means
                to need pride.
                        Mr. Hearst and Marion,
they were nothing like the careless people,
        not the Toms and Daisies that
Fitzgerald writes about.
                        It was only pride for them
if you could *buy* it,
                horde it, everything meticulous,
exact.
        Pride if you could
                crate it up, ship it
        in a hold on some
                        behemoth Great Eastern liner,
each crate marked with a seven-digit number,
                so Mr. Hearst's architects

could erector-set it back
together at San Simeon—
                        Estremaduran monasteries,
Thai pagoda with a gold-leaf peristyle,
        six fake Titians and a bogus Cranach.
                    And Mr. Hearst's menagerie
had *rhinos* aplenty,
                        lyre birds and frigate birds
Galapagos tortoises
                with Edward Evert Horton smiles,
                        a snow leopard cub from Katmandu,
a pair of capybaras christened
                        Eleanor and Franklin.
But Marion drew the line when Mr. Hearst
                arranged to mail her off
                    a clan of twenty
                Congo pygmy warriors—
perfect for the deer park pond, he said.
                Something of a fight ensued
                and Marion won,
                    but not before some half of them
had died of fever, waiting in their crates
                on the docks at Leopoldville. And this
was especially galling to Mr. Hearst.
                After all, he'd *paid* for them.

But I was telling you about pride.
                After Pabst and *Lost Girl* I was poison
                to the studios.
                        But I've written on this
and you know I'd rather write,
                not yammer this way to your little machine.

In 1940 I departed Hollywood forever
                and thought to get away would cure me

of its pestiferous disease,

                referred to even there

as "*going* Hollywood."

                    I retired first to father's

house in Wichita,

           but there I found the citizens could not decide

whether to despise me for having once

                been a success away from home

          or for being now a failure in their midst.

So in '43 I went back to New York

              where I found that the only

well-paying career open to me,

              as an unsuccessful actress of thirty-six,

was that of a call girl.

           You black out your past,

refuse to see your remaining friends,

           you flirt with fantasies

        concerning bottles filled with

yellow sleeping pills.

         And so on.

But I've written about this all before.

           Let me have a cigarette, and I'll give you

something new, something to make

              your article unique.

Dirk of course was not his given name—

        though I can't remember if I even knew

        the real one, Isaac or Jacob

        probably, somewhere from

The Settlement of Pale.

        Nose jobs then

were risky business, but Dirk's was fabulously

        good and aquiline. And I heard

that when the debts came due,

they knew it was the first thing
they should break, along with both his arms.
Our slides, it seems,
ran parallel.
Which brings me to the last time that we met.

They must have refrained from the kneecap routine,
for when I saw him last he was working in
a marathon dance that had come to Wichita.
His second rebuilt nose
was anything but Aryan,
and his suit had been around the block
so much it gave off a sixty-watt shine.
I think the purse was seven hundred,
and when I dropped in it must have been
day thirty-five or thereabouts.
Past midnight the seats went down
from a dollar to ten cents, a place
to go if you couldn't go elsewhere
or if, like me, you couldn't sleep.
They'd bring in a second-string
emcee for the graveyard shift,
mainly there to bait the couples. The orchestra
signed off at one and I
remember the amplified Victrola screeching
"In Old Monterey," "Cielto Lindo,"
then "I Ain't Gonna Cry No More."
And it was Dirk,
Dirk with some floozy big-toothed kid
who couldn't have been much more than seventeen,
a little taller than he was and
a big-boned argument for social
Darwinism, for basically she was holding him up—
if your knees touched the dance floor
you were out—and Dirk was almost down.

88

And it was maybe three — an hour to the
four o'clock ten-minute break.
Mind you, they had a whole
elaborate lingo, special
to the marathon crews. "Goofiness" for when
hallucinations came. And "marathonitis"
when the body simply gave out,
and usually it happened
at times like this, the audience dwindled
down to bums and Edward Hopper whores,
paying mostly just to sleep or heckle.
(And it makes you think of Dante,
doesn't it?) The time they'd label
"The Falling Hour."
This was December, and I can even tell you
that I wore a cheap
red cotton overcoat, having sold
both the furs to get back
to Wichita. So I was shivering,
brushing snow from my collar when I
called
his name, though I don't even know
if he *went* by that name anymore.
But there he teetered
with his big-assed girl, laboring in a *danse macabre*
foxtrot toward me in the stands, and I wish
I could tell you that he said
something clever. But you can imagine
how gallantry comes hard at times like this,
and his eyes were flickering
and his out-of-whack nose seemed to point
due east. *Michelle, this is Louise;*
Louise, Michelle.
How wonderful to see you dear.
We had some good times didn't we.

STUDY SKIN AND AMBERSON

I. FIELD MUSEUM SUBBASEMENT, 1994

O the city of Mahagonny . . .
It should be like a net
Stretched out for edible birds.
—Brecht

The littlest employees weave and chew
and crawl glass walls, the carcasses
of two spotted owls, an autopsied lynx.

There is, of course, the smell, which indicates
industriousness. The raptor eye sockets seethe
with workers, cathedral domes from Piranesi

and Fritz Lang: the tunnels of *Metropolis,*
the Mogli of *The Time Machine.* Dermestid beetles—
they'll strip a carcass in two days, depending

upon size and taste, preferring, says Michael,
mammals to birds. And higher on the food chain,
everyone else is on vacation. The taxidermy desks

abandoned, the AC off and Macs unplugged. So Michael
today plays Carnegie and Samuel Goldwyn,
Thalberg with a studio lot comprised

of seventeen terrariums, Potemkin villages of bone,
of sinew where the cameras hum incessantly.
Clockwise feet race the skulls like nebulae.

Then Michael kills the lights for us.
First the crescendoing smell. And now
from the depths their sound is amplified

to whirlwind, a hundred thousand
minute clicks, psalm of the jaws at work
in unison. Dream City, Night City,

City of Nets. Necropolis awash with song.

. . . in his hotel room watching Ambersons late one evening. The
door was ajar, and as she neared the room she could hear the
voices and see the reflection of the film in the window. She was
about to enter, but stopped.
—*Citizen Welles*

He is weeping on the bed. He is weeping hugely
on the bed. She was about to enter but stopped.
Dark room and the memorizing, chastening light upon

the icehouse scene, refrigerated Sound Stage 4
at RKO. He is weeping on the bed as corn flakes
method act a freezing rain, then snow. *It worried me*

because you couldn't see people's breath.
She was about to enter, but closed the door
and left. "The Man Who Broke the Bank

at Monte Carlo"'s sung, image cloning image—
snow filling screen, and the window's
image of the screen, and the window's image

of the weeping him. And she closes the door,
goes out. . . . In the City of Nets
he is lost. And how to speak of him?

Dropped globe of snow, the shocked entangled hands
constricting Desdemona's throat.
And how to speak of him? . . . The tape I've rented's

colorized, and version three. *I was trying*
to hold on to something, but they . . .
The minutes shaved. One thirty-three

to one one seven, and then the keyboard symmetry
of eighty-eight, inflammable celluloid
like barbershop hair, whisk-broomed in long shot

on RKO linoleum. *Lucy and George for example in
the one-horse open sleigh. And did I tell you how we . . . ?*
The cadaver sewn back up and weeping

hugely. Forensics and the entrails read. Hair, fiber,
semen, blood, but the hair recombed, some rouge
for the cheeks. And how to speak?

Whisk-broomed like barbershop hair,
like the man and his son inching up
a February beach in Provincetown,

their fishtailing truck in the new
wet snow. To beat the Institute for Coastal Studies
team, the Museum of Comparative

Biology. Moonlit low tide, and now
they can reach her, forty feet and tons,
faintly her lavender flanks aglow, already scored

with knife cuts, graffiti. The truck
in the water, up to its doors, and in rubber boots
they wade out to touch her, peel off their gloves

in the headlights' yellow wands of mist,
before the son pulls the chainsaw cord—
recoil and the smell of gas, the father

pointing to the jawline where the son
now aims, sputtering toward the first
of twenty hand-sized teeth. Leviathan

aglow. Leviathan's ivory molars
ensilvered and pulsing in the father's hands,
the tide and the sea's white foam:

the Chinese and the scrimshaw carvers eat them up.

STAMMER

One by one I lift them to the mouth, the tongue
entwining them,
                the five smooth pebbles.

Speak now, speak now, say again.

Let the tongue know its place. This will,
according to Herodotus,
                effect the cure for stammer.

Tongue contra world. Argot and glottal.

And memory, embabeled memory, is here
as well.
            The speech correction teacher Mrs. N

looming back to me this morning as my neighbor

in black spandex cranks her Motown
up to ten, sunshine on a cloudy

day, in her yard as she lifts her hi-tech bow, and then

the target
            bristling arrows. Memory
of the tongue depressor, then its burrow

toward the tonsils. *AH AH AH E E E,*

good David good David good. Stereo
even louder now,
            Tempts, Four Tops

and Miracles, Cloud Nine Standing in the Shadows

of Love. *Talk when I say you can talk.*
Barnyard David barnyard.
                              Bright grail

of *R. R*uth *r*ang *R*andy *r*arely. *Stop.*

Rarely Randy rang. Rarely. Rarely. The stalled
train of the tongue, steaming

engine. Engine on the railroad on the winter trestle

Stalled. But then the grind and hiss and whistling.
I am speaking now I have permission.

Heat Wave, bull's-eye all the arrows bristle,

and she nods to herself. The tongue
set free, the pebbles spit down.

Speak now speak now again again.

Tractate for Doctor Tourette

Therein I clothed myself and ascended.
    —"The Hymn to the Pearl"

The chubby hostess twitches just a little and is smiling while
    she blinks too much.
Smiling while she has us paste the name tags to our chests,
    addresses to be added
to the mailing list. I am not and Michael's not, though Michael's
    dead friend was a *chirper*

and he wants to understand. Little here for poetry: no dead toreadors,
    no Irish patriots,
no Scrabble tiles of severed ears upon the table for effect,
    just brochures, and the mild
surreptitious voyeuristic thrill as we take our seats, await
    the speaker as we scan the crowd

and gratis glossy little booklets jammed with nomenclature:
    chirpers, gulpers, tic-ers,
"scat singers"—as in scatological—the secret protocol
    of touch and probe,
of checking and rechecking in the florid Saint Vitus dance,
    Dionysian marionettes,

but otherwise "completely normal." This is Chicago, no severed ears
    or toreadors and the dead unknowable
and nameless as the living. And our living names already
    obsolescent as dementia praecox,
paraphrenia, catalytic exteriorization phenomena. But Dr. Tourette
    begets a syndrome,

begets the boy in the row before us, his neck abob and twisting
    in a prosody as lost to us

as quantitative meter. And Dr. Tourette's canonical; the rights
      to the boy and every twitch
and *cocksucker motherfuck* and gurgle in the room belong to him.
      He has the movie rights,

has the bag of dried peach halves skittering across the table,
      is Adam and his props.
His props today being our sea of twitches, parting as our speaker
      rises to the crowd,
though he first must stroke the microphone and touch the podium
      seven times. You are of

the mystery, he says, you can't stop its tide, its tic and grimace
      are the wound, and the wound
is the word made flesh. And the sea before him: how it pitches with its
      fingertaps on chair backs,
the clicks and bobs and grunts and flickering compulsive psalmic wails,
      our *this this this*

the undertone and back-up band, this tidal choir which he sings above.
      This is nothing for your poetry.
This is nothing to do with you. Doctor, you are nothing and we are
      not yours. Let the names
be taken back, and in this land our wordless song shall rise,
      its two parts hydrogen,

its one part water, O wordless this, O pearl brought back from Egypt
      to the middle of the sea.

VI

GHOST SUPPER

after Pavese

Under the trellised arbor, and our supper's over
in the memory I've found myself inside.

L not speaking, and beside us the river
sliding softly by. Now the light will fade

to moonlit water. And in memory I work
to make this lingering accurate and sweet.

White ouzo and her hand that lifts the grapes,
first to her lips, then to mine. I may as well speak

to moonlight as to her. And the walls of Bruges
light up again, a costume jewelry pearl string.

Her profile and her shawl hugged tight against the breeze
in memory's flammable celluloid—flaring

and gone, replaced by bread and grapes, a checkered
tablecloth. The two chairs stare each other down,

empty now, upon which moonlight flickered
all night. The bread and grapes drip mist as dawn

carves the morning with a chilly wind,
slicing away both moon and fog. Now someone

without a name appears—first the fevered hands,
Dustdevil quick, that grope for the food in vain.

Then the pale light shows the open mouth
and rippling throat, white face on black water,

sparrow-flock fast, its spiraling path.
But the bread and grapes stay where they were,

their smell tormenting that famished ghost, helpless
to even lick away the dew that gathers

on the grapes, blue fluted sides of the wineglasses.
Dawnlight, everything dripping wet, and the chairs

stare at each other, alone. Sometimes on the riverbank
you can sense an odor—of grapes, or sex, or memory.

It swirls through the moonlit grass. And now wakes
someone always mute, someone without a body

weaving also through the half-lit grass.
The hoarse wail of someone who cannot speak,

who reaches out but cannot *touch* the grass,
and only the nostrils flare. Now the dawn will break,

late autumn cold. To crave so endlessly the warmth—
the blood-pulsing fingertip, the body to embrace,

the pungent smells commingling. To rise like breath
and slither through the trees and tangle every branch

in this unappeasable longing, this endless lust
for touch and smell which afflicts the dead.

The souls in the trees face the gathering light.
Other times, in the ground, the rain torments them.

Dirge and Descent

The Howard Line, the Argyle stop, the window

in "The Window," Little Chinatown.

I'm thinking L on videotape, her final reading, a bow,

then the black rustle of her "reading dress," and down

the proscenium steps. Window and tunnel,

my palm against glass and panic, twisted vision,

noche oscura, el plunging down past Fullerton

like quarters through a turnstile slot, *the shuttle*

to whose winding quest / and passage through these looms

God ordered motion but ordained no rest. . . .

Whirlwind hiss, hip-hop bleeding through some homeboy's headset.

North and Clyborn, Chicago and State, the noir psalm's

ebb and flow, the wheels' scraping ululation.

Where are you now and where am I? The doors blaze open.

APPETITE: BLACK PAINTINGS

Not the Saturn eating eating eating of my friend Tony,
his mad god the father and the father's appetite,
which snarls through his dead son's broken neck,

strips of flesh and blood-fleck down his throat.
Not the Saturn of Seamus Heaney, Madrid-bound and thinking
Ulster. But my own black painting—pointless to tell you

we each find our own. Nineteen eighty-seven,
and every week that fall my walk down Castellano
to the Prado while you write and drink all day

but by Christmas you are sober and can stay that way a year.
Your death takes seven years; my mother's one;
my father's three. The leaves stripped from the trees,

paseo cafés all shut. But from this page today, watching myself
watch myself—that conjured basement room and canvases,
the lighting dim at closing time—I see I go on eating you all,

my appetite insatiable. And where now does it stop?
The gnawing and the ache: my mother's bedside and her cries
are low, the cancer's arabesques so numerous

that X-rays can't pick out the healthy cells. Constrictor mouth,
hugely open. Chew and swallow, the oxygen tank
before me and my father gasping and and and.

Large mouthfuls. The phone line going dead as we talk.
Too drunk to go on you hang up. The helpings towering.
The drawing and the quartering of the hollow bones.

Then the state patrol—*swallow it up*—calling that night
with the news. Mouthful of the personal effects, the purse
gone through and handed me by weary cops. Mouthful of ashes,

mouthful of wax, mouthful of detox squared. And always more
and where does it stop? Swallow there the room
of witches sabbaths, the room of executions

on the third of a long-gone May. Can Saturn
bless Saturn? Can Saturn touch the cheek of Saturn
and lead him to the street, November street

of newsstand, bullfight poster, *Corazon Satanico
con Mickey Rourke?* Can Saturn walk the long paseo,
Inca on pans-pipe and gypsy with goat, *The Herald*

Tribune announcing the dollar's collapse? Can Saturn
ride the ancient festooned cage six flights
to a door which opens to you by lamplight, you

at the desk with the notebook open, his hunger
stilled by that, your face in infinite regression,
looming flaring gold in memory's hall of mirrors?

And here it is over. Here I can stop.

ORACLE

after Plutarch

No, below is water in its form of wind-pummeled cloud.
In fact we are standing on Hurricane Ridge.

And the park service road, whip-snaking below.
The treeline, the sound, and Victoria Island

fifty miles distant into mist. And Ray Carver,
shades on, with Lynda in the photograph,

the three of us posed stiffly. One head taller
than me, he points to a hawk soaring thermals.

And I am the one who can write this.
Flat blue screen, the characters unscroll,

juggled on the laptop all week. The words
are barley cakes, kneaded with honey to appease

the grotto's sacred serpents. You plunge
down a kind of chute, and at the bottom

enter a coffinlike chamber. And now the serpents,
helixing legs and torso, crisscrossing tongues

on fingertip, on nipple. Plutarch reports it:
the shrine set on a mountainside in Thrace

astride a grove, its location still in dispute.
("Look at that hawk," he says, sunglasses off. "She has

a snake in her mouth.") The future was apparently
revealed to initiates in different ways.

Some had visions, others heard voices.
In his poem the future revealed by X-Ray,

so many dark smudges the doctor can't
pick the good cells out. "And I may even

have thanked him habit being so strong."
Grotto or flat blue screen, I wait.

They swallow the barley cakes so delicately,
too dark to see their coloration, skin dry as paper.

Lie here and be still, as the papyri instructs.
The sutures of the head shall part, the soul

spread out like a sail. All the sleeping
bodies below, lit up like islands with soft fire,

assuming first one color, then another.
In the grotto where the vision of them comes to me.

Enclosed in the chamber where the vision of them
living comes to me. Blue screen and never the future.

The vision mostly Lynda, 1985. Scarcely a year,
and the marriage already lost. The cottage

in Port Townsend where we argued that night — recrimination
sharp and flaring like a firecracker string —

almost to dawn. Then the drive to his house
where he'd worked that morning on a poem.

I believe he had stopped writing stories.
Only poems now, and his joy at them.

His study window, bare desk and the sea, how L
told me later she was calmed by that:

"Can we ever learn to live that way?"
And never the future. On his desk

the notebook open, as the morning fog burns off
and in the breeze the pages rustle.

I am the one who can write this.
On my eyelids, flick and burrow of the tongues.

GALLERY IX: A CARVED BONE RING OF CORMORANTS

Edo period, 1650

Under hard yellow light, under glass ablaze
and magnified, shaped and braided into wands,

how calm this surface, drilled and shuffled
into clarity. Yet even clear looks deceive:

this ripple of incision, these hieroglyphs
delicate as wing-beat strokes on snow,

represent instead the word erased, the word
made flesh. Look closer and you see

the real text—a flock of twenty cormorants,
bills linked and circling the hollow bone,

intricate as Kufic script, each one
individual, each hooked bill, each poised

webbed foot, paint-trace and lacquer
forming ebony unblinking eyes, crest and feather,

"no bird larger than one sixty-fourth
of an inch." As if beyond them lay

the untroubled waters of a moonless night,
the wind-bent reeds and pleasure boats,

paper lanterns, the ectoplasmic silk
kimonos of the lords and ladies of the Edo court.

But you have read this carelessly. You must look closer,
read nuance, context, circles within circles: for carved

into every tiny snaking neck's a ring, and though
this ring could fit almost perfectly your lover's wrist,

coolly phosphorescent as it strokes your own,
it is not made for the human hand, but carved

for the cormorant fishermen, to tightly slide
halfway down a cormorant's throat, and to this collar

a leash is attached, so the cormorant becomes
a kind of predatory, living kite, pulled back

to its master with a glistening fish
it cannot swallow. You must think

of Basho's haiku, "Interesting at first, /
then sad, / watching the cormorant-fishing."

Nuance, context, circles within circles:
The sun has left you, the sky is choked with stars.

The night-fishing bird alights, slack leash
pulled taut by the fisherman's hands. My lords,

my ladies, you are watching from the riverbank,
as is the custom on these moonless nights.

You will see me hurl my cormorant, hear wingbeat
and the sharp water-slap as prey is found.

You will, of course, applaud this moment's
evanescent majesty. O distant just Lord,

I will circle and return to you, my neck snapped back,
dark water and the twitch of silver in my mouth.

Before the Words

for Mark Doty

The companion Enkidu is clay. Sharp March dawn
at my study window, at my view of twenty-seven
budless lakefront elms. By May the water vanishes,

blurred green, embowered, lost beyond
the fat arc of the leaves. The companion Enkidu is clay
and not even the godlike Gilgamesh

shall retrieve him from the world below.
I set the book down, to the white cat's
white-noise purr, and half a continent away

my friend wakes alone, to cape light's blue-glass sheen,
and one more morning beyond his lover's death.
There the dog's nails click the wooden floor

and the sun through the curtains
in the hypnagogic dawn begins
its etches and erasures—nightstand, dresser,

photographs, oxeye daisies in a fluted jar.
The bright diagonals lap the room. Is this
how the day prepares its naming, the hesitant tongue

to the gateway of the mouth?
Before the words can be inscribed
they issue from the throat, and song of a kind is invented,

a crumbling harp from the burial pits at Ur,
to testify first to lamentation.
From the throat to the tablets, crosshatched

to point the way, crosshatched in clay and baked
in Euphratian sunlight. The voice
raised first in lamentation, and the voice

entombed, seven hundred generations buried.
But also the voice reborn, its dry bones ablaze.
To cleanse the tablets with a fine horsehair brush

selah. To photograph by silver emulsion
the excavation where they're piled selah. Burnooses
of the grinning fellaheen. To sort the lamentation

onto wooden crates, cataloged and labeled,
hoisted on a river barge for Baghdad, its sky
a hundred years from the black, infernal poppy heads

of antiaircraft fire, elided wail of siren
selah. Istanbul, then London selah or Berlin.
A basement room, the lamentation shuffled

under gas lamps. The sudden pince-nez glint
as Herr Von Dobereiner rubs his eyes,
the inkwell dipped, the letters molten

on the notebook page, unscrolling as the cry
emerges selah from its clay. The Elamite,
the Hittite and the proto-Babylonian,

and the cry as it hovers and its music sweetens.
And the lamentation selah fills the pages,
fills too oh lord the vaulted caverns of the world

below. The companion Enkidu is clay.
Selah selah selah. The tablets have been broken
and the tablets now shall be restored.

"Wreckage": See Kevin Randle and Donald Schmidt, *UFO Crash at Roswell*.

"Among the Joshua Trees": Gram Parsons, who sang with the Byrds and The Flying Burrito Brothers before pursuing a solo career, died of a drug overdose in 1974. His body was stolen by two associates and set afire in the California desert. His posthumous album is entitled "Grievous Angel." The poem is for Rick Madigan.

"4750 Cottage Grove" is for Chris Hull, and was the location of Chess Records' main studio. The Chess roster included Muddy Waters, Howlin' Wolf, Chuck Berry, Little Walter, among others.

"Five Eschatologies": Several members of the Symbionese Liberation Army, political extremists and kidnappers of heiress Patty Hearst, were killed in a shootout with Los Angeles police in 1974. Stephen Jones, son of People's Temple leader Jim Jones, was playing in a basketball tournament in Georgetown, Guyana, on the day of the cult's mass suicide. The Ranters and the Levellers were millenialist anarchistic sects, suppressed by Cromwell.

"The Shades": The poem makes use of material from various sources, especially Edward Candlemass's *Feral Children and Clever Animals*.

"The Nightingales": Nicolae Ceausescu's father also named the future dictator's *brother* Nicholae. A sister, Nicholina, was born later. Alesandro Moreschi was the last great castrati singer. Castrati were often secretly emasculated by their own parents, or by barbers who performed the operation at the behest of the parents: a singing career was seen as one of the few means to escape the poverty of southern Italy. Drone bees, once the queen bee has been impregnated, are expelled from the hive. The ending of the poem owes a debt to Stanley Plumly.

"Elegy and Perisphere" draws from several of my mother's photos of the 1939 New York World's Fair. "Silver Age" is the term used for comic books published during the second great era of comic art, from the early to mid 1960s.

"Lulu in Xanadu" is for Jon Anderson, and makes use of a few phrases from Louise Brooks's *Lulu in Hollywood*. "Tractate for Doctor Tourette" is for Michael Trombley. The epigraph is from the gnostic devotional poem, "The Hymn to the Pearl." "Dirge and Descent" makes use of two lines from Henry Vaughn's "Man."

Thanks to friends for their careful reading of these poems: Tony Whedon, David Jauss, Dean Young, Jim Harms, Mark Doty, William Olsen, Nancy Eimers, and Betsy Sholl. And, to Noelle Watson, the most heartfelt thanks of all.

ACKNOWLEDGMENTS

Acknowledgment is made to the following magazines where certain of these poems appeared, sometimes in earlier versions: *Antioch Review* ("Ode" and "Print Made with Inverted Camera in Situ"); *Black Warrior Review* ("Border Crossings," "Five Eschatologies," "4750 Cottage Grove," and "The Nightingales"); *Chicago Review* ("Cienfuegos Road"); *Green Mountains Review* ("Excavation Photo" and "Lulu in Xanadu"); *Kenyon Review* ("The Shades"); *Michigan Quarterly Review* ("Study Skin and Amberson"); *Missouri Review* ("Among the Joshua Trees," "Elegy and Perisphere," and "In Memory of Primo Levi"); *North American Review* ("Dirge Singing Marianne Faithfull"); *Ohio Review* ("God of Journeys and Secret Tidings"); *Paris Review* ("Before the Words"); *Passages North* ("Truth-Taking Stare"); *Poetry East* ("Appetite: Black Paintings," "Footage and Dirge," and "Tractate for Doctor Tourette"); *Poetry Northwest* ("Gallery IX: A Carved Bone Ring of Cormorants" and "Stammer"); *Quarterly West* ("Wreckage" and "Death and the Maiden"); *Triquarterly* ("After Wittgenstein," "Dirge and Descent," "Hey, Joe," "Oracle," "Rajah in Babylon," and "Speech Grille"); *Yale Review* ("Ghost Supper").

I would also like to thank the National Endowment for the Arts for a fellowship which aided the composition of this book.

DAVID WOJAHN was born in St. Paul, Minnesota, in 1953, and was educated at the University of Minnesota and the University of Arizona. His first collection, *Icehouse Lights*, was selected by Richard Hugo as a winner of the Yale Series of Younger Poets competition and was also chosen as a winner of the Poetry Society of America's William Carlos Williams Book Award. His second collection, *Glassworks*, was published by the University of Pittsburgh Press in 1987 and was awarded the Society of Midland Authors' Award for best volume of poetry to be published during that year. The University of Pittsburgh Press also published his subsequent collections, *Mystery Train* (1990) and *Late Empire* (1994). He has also edited, with Jack Myers, *A Profile of Twentieth Century American Poetry* (Southern Illinois University Press, 1991), and *The Only World*, a posthumous collection of Lynda Hull's poetry (Harper Collins, 1995). He has received fellowships from the National Endowment for the Arts and the Fine Arts Work Center in Provincetown, and in 1987–88 was the Amy Lowell Travelling Poetry Scholar. He has taught at the University of New Orleans, the University of Houston, and the University of Arkansas at Little Rock. He presently teaches at Indiana University and in the MFA in Writing Program of Vermont College. He lives in Chicago.